500
HAIKU

JASON HANRAHAN

ISBN: 9798768211578

Paperback

000000002

By the same author:

Haiku Dreams. A personal haiku journal with images and commentary.

This book is dedicated to my friend Paul Stephen, who is far more spiritual and Zen than I will ever be.

Contents

Introduction

I have to confess that for much of my time on this rotating rock in space, the art of haiku had largely passed me by. Poetry (and a great deal of art) I would mostly dismiss as pretentious nonsense (or often something less polite!!!) I vaguely remember covering haiku in haste in school perhaps aged about 12 years old, but little more. More recently a friend who is a fabulous baker and photographer would enhance her mouth wateringly gorgeous images of buns, cakes and cookies lightly dusted with icing sugar on Facebook with deep and meaningful haiku verses. My interest was piqued.

I have always had a fascination for Japanese culture, initially as a result of the influence of manga and anime, but later through a growing interest in bonsai and koi keeping. This introduced me to phrases such as "wabi-sabi" and Zen. I am also a voracious reader, and often read over a hundred books each year, and my attention has recently turned to Japanese literature, Zen writings and the Japanese classics. Recently this has covered **The Tale of Genji**, **Travels with a Writing Brush, One Hundred Poets, One Poem Each**, **Zen Fool Ryokan** and **Essays in Idleness** amongst others. It was only a matter of time before I would find myself absorbing the works of haiku masters such as Buson, Basho, Issa and Ryokan. With their beautifully poetic sense of transient beauty, something inside me was awakened.

For me, a haiku represents a snapshot in time, a vignette perfectly captured in minimalistic language. It conjures a vivid image and evokes an emotive response. Similarly, a beautiful image or photograph can tell a powerful story through lighting, framing and composition. Indeed, a picture paints a thousand words. It seemed natural to combine the two to generate a powerful reaction. The limitations of the form also appeal to me as an intellectual challenge, a word game used to demonstrate wit and wisdom. It is playful. It is joyous.

Amongst my reading were also books on happiness, and a key learning was simply finding things to be grateful for. Some suggested writing a list every day, or telling people how much you appreciate them. To be thankful for the beauty around us, for the small things that we might otherwise miss in the rush of our busy lives. Out of this sentiment sprang my haiku journal, a tattered notebook where I scribble my thoughts. Strictly speaking it includes not only haiku in the classic sense, but also senryu – like haiku but a more satirical commentary on people, politics, society.

The haiku included here are the direct results of a conscious effort to be more mindful and Zen, to appreciate wabi sabi and the beauty and impermanence of the little things, to be thankful every day. They were written during 2020, a year much marred by the worldwide Covid-19 pandemic, as will be evident from several of the verses. My partner has often had to patiently stand by as I pause in the middle of a country walk to compose a verse and check it's syllable count on my mobile phone. I don't claim to be a great poet, but on the principle that if you throw enough stuff at the wall some of it may stick, I simply wrote and wrote and wrote. In the middle of work, whilst commuting, in the dark hours in the middle of the night when I couldn't sleep, or the stillness of the morning listening to the dawn chorus. Whenever inspiration struck, I recorded my thoughts in my haiku journal.

Composing these haiku and senryu gave me great personal pleasure and satisfaction, and I hope that some of that can be imparted to you as reader.

I humbly thank you for taking time to indulge me, and to read this work. May you too find reason to be thankful every day.

Jason Hanrahan
November 2021.

The Haiku

Cherry blossom stirs
Dappled light on mossy stone
Too transient beauty

Soft wind stirred chimes.
Gentle music of the spheres -
Sings to my essence

Radiant sunlight
In a shimmering raindrop -
Rainbow colour wash

Graceful grey heron
Perched regally, high above
Eyes my precious koi.

Recipe abused,
Chocolate muffins sunken,
Partner unimpressed.

Miserable rain,
Dark cloud filled skies above me.
Shitey Brit summer.

Bright sunny morning.
Camera records the scene.

Three points on licence.

Fierce radiant orb,

In a cloudless azure blue.

Enraptures my soul.

I am most humbled

Your praise appreciated.

Oh queen of haiku.

Lush grassy meadow.

Fronds sway in soft summer breeze.

Bug bitten ankles.

Glittering green eyes,

Warm, soft, downy fur humming.

Cuddles with my cat.

Miniature trees.

Contorted by hand and wire.

"Natural" beauty.

A trilling thrush sits

Amid red rowan berries.

Swoops low and is gone.

Onwards ever up.
Legs tremble under dark boughs.
Summit - heart attack!!!

Sea spray splashed rock.
White caps on roiling grey waves.
A lonely gull cries.

Let down by colleagues
My fears made reality
Manager's burden

Secret Santa fun
My colleagues don't much know me
They are all Muslim

Haiku distractions
Witticisms and wise word play
Real work is postponed

Rods of cool, fresh rain:
A sudden summer shower
Soon over. Lush green grass

Mournful calls of "Dave",
"Dave". A heart breaking chorus

From a field of sheep.

Tendrils of blue smoke
A pleasing incense inhaled
Soothes weary spirit.

Evening sunlight rays
Sets fire to glowing leaf
Gold, amber and green

Welcome to the internet.
Brings out the best in people
And the very worst.

Swallows whirl and dance
Cotton clouds in azure sky
Framed by my window.

Lawnmowers whirring
Outside my office window
My life in lockdown

Yellow eye in pond
Floats amid green lily pads
Then too soon is gone

Daylight creeps over
A sleeping world Is revealed
Ghostly world recedes

Stillness hangs over
A ghostly world in slumber
Birds begin to chirp

Sun stirs gentle mist
Across a lake serenely
A new day begins

Horse chestnut bonsai
Conquer growing habit, leaves
Like dinner plates

Koi splash playfully
A buddha sits serenely
In the dappled shade

Green Foliage stirs
Cat approaches stealthily
Hisses and cat slaps.

Big blousy flowers
Large white and yellow trumpets

Sway in the warm breeze

Upon stirring sea
Of yellow mustard flowers
The sun sinks westward

A soothing hot bath
To ease off the working day
On my own clock now

Silence and greyness
The office: end of lockdown
Desks still and empty

Cerise coloured skies
The sun's last rosy kisses
As daylight recedes

Oh Queen of Haiku
you created a monster
In three lines of verse

I hope to find peace
But find it just too tacky
In this Happy Land

I hope to find Zen
But it smells of hot dog food
In this Happy Land

Through duck weed peering
On balmy summer evening
Tiny frog bathing

A sleeping cat
Paws twitching for
Invisible mice

A black butterfly
Fancy phantom flutterer
transiently ghosts by

A haze of blue fog
On a warm summer evening
Smells like sausages

Busy workers pass
Amid the drying grasses
Ant society

Serene old pond
A fish leaps out

Plop! Ripples recede

Amid lily pads
Red, white and yellow fish feed.
A bird sings proudly

My green tea whisk stand:
Sleeks, shiny, jade ceramic
Looks like a butt plug.

Only silence now
Where once chicks were hatched and raised
Shit on bay window

Gold and rust brown leaves
Hiss like paper in the breeze
Winter approaches

A petulant child
Cries with sad howls of anguish
This, my neighbour's dog

Fluffy little clouds
Swallows darting after flies
Soon will fly southward

Bracken surrounds me
A half imagined footpath
This Hell of Horcum

Horcum water falls
A steaming stream of yellow
from a cow's behind

Tiny insect crawls
Across a page of verse.
Enjoying haiku?

Uneven blue glaze
My favourite bonsai pot
So wabi sabi

Slim blue leaves stirring
In the gentle midday breeze
butterfly flits by

Lovely sunny face
Atop a slender green stalk
Reflects the fierce sun

An old bird warbling
Through the dark and misery

C'est La vie en Rose

Dead branch amid green
My neighbour hired
Tree butchers not surgeons

Dead branch amid green
My neighbour seems to have hired
Butchers not surgeons

Such wit and wisdom
In seventeen syllables
I love a Haiku

A picture painted
In seventeen syllables
I love a Haiku

Silent shadows scud
Across a verdant valley
Occupied by sheep

On my commute:
Black sheep doing yoga
On a grassy knoll

Bathed in hot water
Watching leaves sway overhead
Clear Summer evening

Bathed in hot water
Watching birds wheel overhead
Clear Summer evening

Seen from my hot tub
A Japanese lantern sits
By a still koi pond

A placid koi pond
Reflects a silvery sky
Birds reel overhead

Sing your proud heart out
Robin, bobbing on the fence
A rare treat for cats

Lazy Sunday noon
Rain drums conservatory roof
Cat washes her face

Amid a jungle
Of fronds I sit and read

A lazy Sunday

A Buddha beneath
A towering banana tree
Just like Basho?

Does our Monarch think
The whole world smells like fresh paint?
Asking for a friend

Big Issue seller
Gives the world a toothy grin
A smile costs nothing

Like swift silver darts
And elegant wafting fans
I watch my koi swim

Swiftly beating heart
Within a mass of feathers
Fly free little bird

Tiny beating heart
Nestled safely in my hand
Fly free little bird

Cotton candy clouds
Float in a silver blue sky
Moisture on the breeze

Majestic tree boughs
Leaves dangling in the warm breeze
Robbed of your beauty

A vat of koi fry
A tiny net determines
Whether life or death

Forever onward
Always shorter than one thinks
Life's transient journey

A garden of trees
A forest of slender boughs
In elegant pots

Kite tails fluttering
Soaring like a dancing bird
A child's joyous face

Kite tails fluttering
Flapping like a dancing bird

Children on a hill

Proud flower beware!
Beauty amid the grasses
Mower approaches

Wind stirring the trees
Waving and swaying like limbs
Autumn approaches

Scrawny ancient cat
Blackened lips, unsteady legs
Summer days must end

Our time is so short
Seasons in the shifting rain
Kindness costs nothing

Our time is so short
Blown about by season's winds
Kindness costs nothing

Be grateful daily
Dancing in the summer rain
Waters the spirit

How the years fly by
He doesn't recognise me -
Man in the mirror

Lamenting lost youth
The old man in the mirror
Reflects life like mine

Their daily commute
Busy rushing to and fro
Colony of ants

Canaries can wait
Patience being a virtue
In pandemic times

Just like my mother's:
A cake baked with love
Burnt, inedible

Dappled canopy
Questing beams of sunlight
Probe the forest floor

Dappled canopy
A probing beam of sunlight

Strobes the forest floor

Every image lost
Distilled moments of beauty
Like tears in rain

Rods of cold rain fall
Heavy from a leaden sky
Coffee warms my hands

After the rain falls
Lightening skies, renewed hope
The grass still wet though

This book of faces
Makes none a better version
Unlike a real book

This book of faces
Makes none a better person
It's not a real book

Shower him in gold
This narcissist President
Stormy times ahead

Is that a bad wig
On orange man-baby's head?
Concealing no brain!

The meaning of life
To be happy and healthy
Perhaps forty two

An orange baboon
In a tacky gold White House
So much Covfefe

An orange baboon
In a tacky gold White House
It seems hate Trumps love

A vignette painted
In seventeen syllables
God loves a trier

A silent old pond
A weighted body thrown in
Silence. Might be best

Towering mountain
Dreams of reawakening

Beneath the black waves

Mountain that walked
Sleeping in his charnel house
Dreams insanity

Morning stillness hangs
Upon a world bathed in sun
Hope again renewed

A golden dawn breaks
Endless possibilities
The sleeper awakes

Struts like a proud king
Radiant regal magpie
Feathers green and blue

Ancient castle walls
Glimpsed through the dappled trees
One man's folly

Massive ancient tree
Gnarled limbs reaching for the sun
Marking years like hours

A flower garden

Beds of radiant colour

Pensioners planted

In Twenty Twenty

The radicalised Reich wing

Trumps America

A Haiku posted

Glowing plaudits are received

Ego monster born

Through this thoughtful praise

A monster was created.

Damn pride and ego

Afternoon's sun glow

Bathing everything in warmth

Inspires lethargy

Playful splash and roll

A fishy feeding frenzy

The sun falls westward

Sequins and prancing

Not Strictly for everyone

Stick it up your arse

Dimpled down under
Four thousand pounds of beauty!
What a silly arse

Not even pale moon
Lights this still, midnight blackness
Sleep so evasive

A thunderous clock
Steals these precious hours of sleep
Still Blackness outside

Drinking cherry tea
As around me others sleep
Midnight blackness rules

The kitchen clock ticks
Measures out every second
As others slumber

Sleep impossible
With your head an airless box
These first world problems

It spirals beyond
The murder, madness, mayhem
As Great Cthulhu dreams

A bronze leaf tumbles
Turns in the golden sunlight
A chill in the air

A bronze leaf tumbles
Turns in the golden sunlight
Autumn's harbinger

Rows of tiny trees
A forest in my garden
In ceramic pots

A field with no sheep
Like farmers without wellies
Each to his own (kind)

It knows your full name
And your most inner desires
Careless talk costs lives

It knows your full name
And your most secret desires

Your id up for sale

Little furry gifts
Don't think that I'm ungrateful
Presents from my cat

Healing frequency
A softly purring engine
Cuddles with my cat

Red fiery orb sinks
Beyond undulating waves
But not on flat Earth

On this spheroid Earth
Some people think it is flat
Some brains must be too

Keep writing they said
Persevere as well they said
Look who's laughing now!

Gazing at us from
The near dim and distant past -
Ghosts, old photographs

Moments caught in time
We will never see their like
Faces in photos

Watching reactions
As a car injures a child
Speed awareness course

Year end approaches
Pleased to see the back of
This pandemic year

New Year approaches
All hope it is better than
This pandemic year

This is no spider
Paternal or otherwise
This leggy crane fly

No daddy long legs
Identity confusion
This is a crane fly

Unknown flying craft
As flown by little grey men

Probably Russian

Strange lights in the sky
Forms not from around this way
Probably marsh gas

Wreckage at Roswell
What a load of dummies
Weather balloon crash

Better than tv
Watching koi roll, splash and play
Earthly paradise

Furious tweeting
Hidden up amongst the trees
There's no Twitter here

In the azure skies
Lines fading, dissipating
Memory of a jet

Wishing you were here
You cannot come soon enough
Twenty twenty one

Yellow sun ascends
On ceaseless rolling water
A sunrise at sea

All nonsense believed
Nothing is off the table
Conspiracy nuts

Sinking slowly down
Towards the sombre tree line
Early autumn sun

Wheels of golden straw
All lined up across a field
The autumn harvest

They have hate for those
Who do not speak their language
Or better than them

Today not sailing
Across the Bay of Biscay
Weather terrible

Passing through Dartmoor
They shoot horses don't they?

We all have to eat

All nonsense believed
Nothing is off the table
Q must be joking

In Barnard Castle
For an eye test? Cannot see
Dominic Cummings

You cannot sit there
An abundance of caution
Much thanks to covid

Concrete Human zoo
Young Offenders Institute
Don't feed the animals

Livestock grazing in
A patchwork of green and brown
Cool rain drifts across

Corner of a field
Walls defying gravity
A ramshackle hut

Rolling cloud obscures

Where cows and sheep stand grazing

Damp and verdant fields

The trouble I've seen

Nobody knows but Jesus

Not entirely true

White cloud drifts over

A dark and sombre mountain

A still lake reflects

Looming out the mist

Dark, pine tree covered mountains

White sheep bathed in dew

You can't spell "hatred"

It's a universal fact

Without "red" and "hat"

Heads amongst the clouds

With feet planted on firm ground

Vast dreaming mountains

Mist shrouded mountains

Filling grey horizons, dream

For eternity

In such a hurry
To kill or maim each other
Knobs on country roads

In amongst the trees
Mangled wreckage of a car
Drivers aren't pilots

Horror realised:
Let monstrous sleeping gods lie
Beneath ceaseless waves

Cries of whiney brats
Haunt English Heritage sites
Adult only days?

Sat beneath a tree
Is the soundtrack to my hell
Other people's kids?

Scan this QR code
Before you can come inside
Luddites are exempt

Sometimes it feels like
The path you're on is uphill
In both directions

It can move mountains
Or fly planes into buildings
Faith works such wonders

Is "wabi sabi"
The reason why I so loved
The second Death Star?

Week two not sailing
Round the Canary Islands
Weather picking up

Brain freeze not likely
When eating frozen ice cream
If you have no brain

The sun greets the day
Waves wash gently over sand
Tall ship at anchor

A cloud enveiled sun
Kisses undulating waves

A new day begins

By a glassy lake
I sit in contemplation
Still waters run deep

Masks Worn everywhere
Obsessive washing of hands
COVID damn panic

Tendrils drift across
White, creeping, living, breathing
Cornish moorland mist

Waves ceaselessly wash
Over a white shingle beach
Worries come and go

Thick sea mist conceals
A stunning scenic view
Bay of St Ives

Depression descends
Future becomes uncertain
Covid surges back

A lioness roar

Tiny woman in black robes

Ruth Bader Ginsberg

Seasons cycle on

Like hand removed from water

The ghost that was you

Shadows dance on stone

They stir in celebration

Last days of summer

A cool grey zephyr

Carries moisture in the air

Reflects my grey mood

A cold, driving rain

Lashes down, stinging my eyes

Is the sky crying

A cold, driving rain

Lashes down, stinging my eyes

I am not crying

Restless, sleepless nights

How it interrupts my dreams

This COVID nightmare

Occupied by ghosts
Empty chairs at empty desks
Office in lockdown

Hard working from home
Perfectly manicured lawns
Netflix and chilling

Each single vision
Private, personal, unique
Be grateful each day

Each precious moment
Only you experienced
You take it with you

Golden light recedes
As I sit gently reading
Nearby koi are feeding

Truly makes no sense
Abducting trees from the wild
Would be vandalism

A lunch on the go
Is only convenience food
If you can catch it

He vents his spleen
This is quite an achievement
Thanks to the transplant

Curtains subtle twitch
Eyes watching my every move
Nosey cat observes

Online banking help
Enough to make you see red
Give you no credit

Online banking help
Enough to make your blood boil
Not much help at all

Her sensitive soul
Bared on social media
Perils of Facebook

"No more fish" he said
"The pond overstocked" he said

"Hello my pretties!"

Purple pagoda
Temple to nature's beauty
I pay my respects

It defies logic
Trolley loads of toilet roll
COVID Panic buy

Does she dream of me
The faithful love of my life?
My beautiful cat

Burning sensation
Painful stinging when passing water
Seems you're in trouble

Places we didn't see
Memories we didn't make
Lamenting a cruise

City on the sea
Memories we didn't share
We will meet again

We're sorry to hear
Your holiday was cut short
By your death at sea

Friends who never met
Do they really exist?
Only on Facebook

Each single being
Every single living soul
All dust in the wind

Each single being
That ever walked the earth
All dust in the wind

Often things unplanned:
Moments arise unbidden
Out of the ether

Is it uniform
Grubby grey, unwashed sweat pants
Underemployed youth

Skeletal fingers
Clawing at leaden grey sky

Rotting tree remains

You cannot stand there
Oblivious to others
Causing obstruction

Breaking the silence
Raucous laughter of ducks
Must be my bad jokes?

Breaking the silence
Loud raucous laughter of ducks
Gulls hysterical

Youthful pale skin marked
Ruptured, creased by passing years
Ageing leaves it's mark

Earth bound tentacles
Life sustaining mossy limbs
Ancient tree roots

In far ancient times
Did they hold such mystery
Stonehenge monoliths

Uneven slabs cross

A lazy flowing river

Life ebbs slowly by

Prehistoric tourists

Did they bring their own

Pre-packed lunches

All things are transient

Nothing can last forever

Except perhaps death

Move along the bus

Make some more room for others

A baby is born

Remember me for

The size of my immense heart

And not my ego

Not voting Trump today

His failings run so deep

No U.S. citizen

Presidential debate

Like watching mud flinging in

An old folks care home

The things you most love
No cast iron guarantees
They return your love

The things you most love
No matter how hard you try
They all go away

Excuse me I see
Your pond filled with rock and plants
Hard water issues?

So the poop was flung
No knockout blow was landed
Trump's mic not switched off

In the age of Trump
Americans overseas
Fake Canadians

Hazy afternoon
Lazily lulled to sleep by
The wood pigeon call

Dew drops sparkling
The world stirring to life
A new day begins

Sunlight enraptured
In diamond sparkling dew
A new day begins

A carpet of dew
Sparkling diamond droplets
Reflect rising sun

They watch me pissing
Mother and child spying on
My private moments

As daylight seeps in
Cold rain drums upon the roof
Lamenting summer

A heavy grey still
Rests oppressively upon
A world at slumber

Morning rain stirs me
From dull and anxious dreaming

A grey day begins

Yellow flowers grow
Where once soldiers fought and died
Time subdued them all

I stare sadly at
A chocolate bar wrapper
Funny how things go

Rain falls on a pond
As carp glide slowly by
Nice weather for ducks

Sultan to the Prince:
"Monkeys in a gilded cage
Don't eat all at once"

Dull ape in a mask
May look somewhat ludicrous
Less likely to spread

Ignore health warnings
At super spreader events
Trump's America

In a dense reed bed
A heron sits patiently
Death does not hurry

Runs rings around me how
This mask-less orange ape
I've never seen Trump run

It's not for ever
It's just for now. Mask, wash, space
COVID precautions

"Maybe I'm immune
Must be due to my great genes"
"Will you just shut up"

Seen From my window
Eucalyptus branches wave
A cold wind stirring

Childhood accident
Is my life now just images
In a flash forward?

House martins have gone
They no longer wheel and dive

The sky is bereft

Other people's kids
Sometimes ugly little things
Best to hold your tongue

Someone has to love
These ugly little monsters
Other people's kids

Sun's rays warm my face
A pause, welcome reprieve from
Autumns march onward

White water cascades
Foams and tumbles over stone
Catching golden sun

Leaden skies threaten
Rumours of rumbling thunder
Moisture on the breeze

Leaden skies threaten
Rumours of rumbling thunder
Tension in the air

Circles in circles
Within circles in a square
Rainfall on the pond

Only ruins now
Where brothers once slept and worked
Dark rooks cross the sky

Two sphinxes staring
A century they played this game
Both have yet to blink

The surface serene
Many struggles go unseen
Reflecting real life

An old man stooping   .
Four centuries he has stood
Venerable oak

Clinging on for life
Exposed limbs grasping at rock
Twisted cliff top tree

Fiery orange glow
Trees in fierce autumn colour

Wind stirs fallen leaves

Sunlight refracted
Glistening diamond dew
A chill in the air

A flaming hillside
Alight with orange, reds and gold
Autumn finery

This rich man's folly
Temple to excess and wealth
Built on slavery

Rosy orange skies
Greet the slowly dawning day
Autumns final flush

Pale orange street lights
Punctuate cold morning mist
Fox crossing the road

Get a load of that
Fresh country air fills your lungs
Smells of cow manure

In a leafy glade
Bright red agaric mushrooms
Fairy parasols

Books on books on books
On top of books on more books
Must stop buying books

Relentlessly on
Page by page ever upwards
I climb book mountain

Leaves crunch under foot
Summer has left the building
Say hello to fall

Autumn's rosy kiss
Leads delicate leaves to blush
Pride before the fall

Halloween season
Keep your disease to yourselves
Foul little monsters

Lost in silent grief
He stands beside the grave where

Once he was buried

My grocery list
However so lyrical
Is not a haiku

Gently humming with
The frequency of healing
Cuddles and cat hugs

In thick morning mist
Coughing shadows pass me by
My breath a small cloud

Looming from the mist
Coughing shadows pass me by
Corona virus threat

Pale sun breaking through
Autumnal gold canopy
Cold stillness abounds

A view from a hill
Wind stirred lake surface
Shimmering sunlight

Praying it will stop
Watching Strictly Come Dancing
Poncing in sequins

Natures finest gold
Nestling in the roots of trees
Crisp fallen leaves

Leaf falls in the woods
Is it very like the sound
Of one hand clapping

Almost forgotten
In a tangled knot of trees
Dark stone obelisk

Decency won out
We can take a breath again
Love in fact Trumps hate

Dark windows like eyes
Staring from a brooding hall
Haunted by it's past

A chance encounter
Not all new friends have two legs

Parting is sorrow

No one now alive
Can remember who they were
Toppled grave markers

Follow the leader
Here's hoping he knows the way
Birds migrating South

Ankle deep in mud
I climb this hill on my knees
And down on my arse

Pale sun sinks westward
Autumn's finery now spent
A chill in the air

Skeletal tree forms
Silhouettes against grey skies
Steady cold rain falls

Between bare branches
Lacy cobwebs hung with dew
Catch blazing sunlight

Early morning hush
World bathed in sodium light
The clock ticks loudly

So the saying goes
A cat may look at a king
Same goes for sunrise

In a wooded glade
Dancing with weird abandon
White hooded figures

Amongst the reed beds
The only thing twitching
Is my restless legs

On a country walk
It saddens my heart to see
Dog poo tree in fruit

Deserted quarry
Quiet now where witches danced
With wild abandon.

If I set a trap
Will you blunder into it?

Now over to you...

In a wooded dell
Twisted tree limbs reaching out
Could it be magic

Rusty brown oak leaves
Rustling like dry paper
Gathered in puddles

Snuggling warm beneath
A cosy winter blanket
Though heating is on

Praying to Santa
These dyslexic Satanists
Though neither exist

Life's balancing act
When fickle fate hands you rocks
Why not make rock stacks

Ionic temple
So much more money than sense
Vanity project

Blazing larch tree leaves
Against the dark bare woodland
Fiery autumn gold

Against cold grey skies
A tracery of fine branches
A lone crow laments

Corner of a park
She weeps deeply for spring
Leafless silver birch

Bright winter berries
Vivid warm colours amid
The seasonal grey

A constellation
Each one dazzling and brilliant
We are made of stars

A lonely light house
Bastion against the dark
Shining beacon home

Trilling in a tree
Singing his tiny heart out

Red breasted robin

This covid season
Exuberant Christmas cheer
Stick it up your arse

You come from nothing
Live a brief but frantic life
Then back to star dust

At the end of life
What rich stories you could tell
If you were not dead

Lost in the forest
Amid bare trunks I wander
My Zen place of calm

They hunt together
These sleek creatures honed to kill
For Dreamies cat treats

A gift from the stars
Mysterious monolith
Aliens use rivets?

In another age
Loving arms would hold you safe
Now just memories

Snow blanketed world
Christmas card perfect image
Sheep seem unimpressed

Crisp frozen snowfall
Cracks and crunches underfoot
Red faces, numb hands

Call me Frankenstein
New life contrived in a tank
Hello Sea Monkeys

Season finale
A deadly new strain emerges
Covid mutated

Pointlessness writ large
Japanese literature
Mountains from molehills

Ash rains from the sky
Grazed knuckles covered with blood

Each has a story

In her finery
She refuses to sleep
Japanese maple

Festive carols sung
Crackling log in the fireplace
Christmas screen saver

A brass band plays
Caught on security cam
Christmas cheer abounds

Faint sound of sleigh bells
Heavy footsteps on the roof
Children slumber on

Sat amid the snows
A flushed pink princess blushes
Maple still in leaf

Drumming on the stairs
The thunder of tiny feet
Cats playing at tig

A warm orange glow
Cast across grey cloud blankets
Christmas Eve sunrise

Muddy footprint trail
All about the unlit fire
Not Santa but cats

A gentle pink blush
Spreads across a winter sky
Merry Christmas all

My life haunted by
Dreams of things I never did
A lot like sleeping

Climbing from the soil
Like a huge splayed octopus
Gnarly grey tree roots

A grey winter day
We still commemorate them
And their sacrifice

Delicate petals
Stirred by a chilling breeze

Pink winter cherry

Silent snow falling
Blankets a world in slumber
Coffee warms my hands

They snuggle tightly
World sleeps under snow blankets
Winter coldness bites

Forest canopy
Trees stand white beneath fresh snow
Bonsai in winter

"Are you coming now?"
Question asked in urgency
"Momentarily"

It has hidden depths
And can leave a nasty taste
Beware yellow snow

Fierce battle rages
Casualties on both side
Wintery snowball fight

Against leaden skies
Boughs festooned with crisp white snow
A lone crow heads home

Through banks of soft snow
Tender grass stems reach for light
Life always persists

White snow laden fields
These hedges march forever on
Whatever weather

Wintery paradise
This garden created with love
Snow, bonsai and koi

On their lofty perch
These sea pigeons warm their feet
"No snow up here mate"

Snow and silence now
Where once the witches danced
Too cold for Sabbath

They drive like madmen
Morons in expensive cars

On wintery roads

Does he feel the cold
This writhing twisted old man
An ancient oak tree

A world turned white
Virgin snows crunch underfoot
A cold north wind blows

Footprints in the snow
Mark the course of busy lives
Not all are human

The hard icy ground
Cracks and crunches underfoot
Beneath frosted trees

Sunlight weakly probes
Through bare twisted, frosted boughs
Woodland in winter

Slender white beauty
Stands amid the frozen snows
Regal silver birch

Glittering diamonds
Sit atop the frozen snow
Frosted ice crystals

See her resting now
Her eighty year reign over
Fallen silver birch

They huddle for warmth
Tender kissing silver trunks
Even trees know love

Silver and diamonds
Adorn their finest garments
Majestic birch trees

No cream or cure
Will revive her faded beauty
Ruptured old birch bark

White blindness descends
Snowfall obscures everything
Traffic crawls slowly

White water rushing
Sluicing, splashing over rock

Memories of snow

Life boils and bubbles
Thrives in primordial soup
Want bread rolls with that?

Society sleeps
Isolates and hibernates
Better times will come

Washington on fire
Flames of outrage fanned by
A vile orange ape

Capitol idea
Idiotic President
Pours petrol on the flames

A pale sun rises
Yellow light greets the new day
Captured in ice gems

Clear blue skies belie
The bitter cold of Winter
Icy underfoot

Cars on icy roads
Where are they all going to
In this new lockdown

Smouldering away
Amid the crisp snowy fields
Steaming pile of sh!t

Under frosted boughs
Powdery snows still falling
Despite the noon sun

Snow frosted forest
Picture postcard perfection
Winter wonderland

Against frozen snows
Yellow gorse shining like gold
Defiant flower

Radiant glory
A splash of vibrant colour
Bright winter berries

Falling into light
Golden rays envelop me

As the world rotates

Velvet moss glistens
Red fronds salute the sun
Soft sound of birdsong

When it's all over
Amongst the memories this:
Discarded face masks

Whispy stream of cloud
Flowing through an azure sky
No sound but birdsong

If a snow flake falls
In the forest of the night
No one hears it scream

Burdened with snow
Is not my usual view
Eucalyptus tree

Gold coins free to all
At the end of the rainbow
Kill a leprechaun

A new day dawning

Reflecting on past mistakes

Hope for the future

Dark shadows huddled

Across a silent landscape

New moon's sideways smile

Amid frozen trees

I sit, breathe and contemplate

The nature of truth

In a briar patch

He sits still and watches me

Red breasted robin

Air of reverence

Tranquility created

By soft candle light

This dry cough of mine

Is nothing so serious

No need to panic

Your palpable fear

There's no need to back away

I only coughed

They whirl and cavort
In a droplet of water
Microscopic beasts

It's a foolish thing
To revere any mortal
As purely divine

Microbial life
On the face of a pebble
Human existence

A radiant glow
Feel the heat kissing your face
The sun's warm embrace

A radiant glow
Feel the heat kissing your face
Goodbye possessions

I greatly admire
Your green verdant velvet sleeve
Moss enveloped branch

In decades from now
This featureless Hornbeam stump
Will be fine bonsai

In the bitter cold
The frost rimed grass so sublime
No-one to see it

This ramshackle ruin
It's untended garden now
Is home to fox cubs

Keeps them all awake
Palindromic theorists
This: Do geese see god?

Soft pink confetti
Falling to the grass beneath
the old cherry tree

At the death of spring
Walking on a carpet of
Pink cherry blossom

In afternoon glare
Past the hazy fields of wheat

The silvery moon

They gently caress
The lapping, cooling waters
Weeping willow leaves

The healing power
Of a child's gleeful laughter
Given most freely

A silence descends
In large white snowflakes flurries
The world slumbers on

In a crowded room
Taking nervous sips of wine
Rather than engage

Tendrils of thick smoke
Man intruding my bedroom
Nocturnal terrors

Withered Christmas wreath
Hanging from the flaking door
Almost four months old

House in sparkling lights
A festive feast to behold
In early August

Newly seeking work
Will consider anything
Excepting real work

Road goes ever on
Of this I am quite certain
Though I can't see it

From out of the fog
To the surprise of us both
A startled pheasant

In the dark small hours
I lay awake and listen
To the sound of rain

On the carpet now
Matted balls of fur and bile
Presents from my cat

Apex predator
Vicious killer honed for death

Sleeps the day away

Watery Yellow

Golden sunlight through grey cloud

Reflected on snow

Iron frozen hills

Recede into cold distance

My breath a white cloud

Cold gnaws my fingers

On a frigid winter morn

Ground hard as iron

On a frozen lake

Once the island home to herons

Long deserted now

By a copse of trees

He meditates serenely

Chromatic buddha

Fearful geometry

Amid the trees darkly squats

Mossy pyramid

This gigantic bird
Always remains the same size
Despite the ice cold

Source of my troubles
All the problems I can see
And ones I cannot

Intense love for you
Expressed as plastic roses
From a petrol station

Starry winter skies
Underneath Orion's Belt
Orion's trousers

Silvery moon light
Undulates in gentle waves
Pale cherry blossom

Under moonlit skies
It is snowing soft pink flakes
Cherry blossom ghosts

Sharing my cold bed
With the bitter ghost of you

Through the longest nights

Laid beside his wife
In a busy hospital
Even beyond death

Black fleeting vision
Life in fear amongst the weeds
A baby goldfish

Days getting longer
Conceivably explains why
I feel so exhausted

Grey jumble of rock
Is a Japanese garden
It won't build itself

This jumble of wood
Is a Japanese tea house
It won't build itself

Celestial light
Bathing in your ghostly glow
Wintery Snow moon

Three in the morning
Each restless waking second
Is ten minutes long

Paint paint paint paint paint
Paint paint paint paint paint paint paint
Paint paint paint paint done

My heart sings to see
Long forgotten friends returned
First cherry blossom

A golden sunrise
To the sound of dawn's chorus
And soft pigeon calls

Late in the garden
The blackbird sings his sweet song
To the setting sun

When the work is done
Time to enjoy peace and rest
In the Zen garden

Birds twitter and tweet
In darkness even the sun

Is still fast asleep

Beneath red maples
Dappled sunlight dancing on
Verdant velvet moss

Poo on the knuckles
How's that even possible
Asking for a friend

Leaning on his stick
Bears the weight of aged limbs
Gnarly old oak tree

Biting mosquito
In a previous life may
Have been my mother

Absorbed in his work
Too occupied with blossom
To acknowledge me

Dawn chorus in dark
The moon dances on the pond
Beneath the cascade

Even beyond death
Body resting in the ground
The bank gets it's share

As the Buddha said
Attachments bring such sorrow
Same true of email

Beneath Easter skies
A whispy cloud of sheep drifts
Across a green field

A gentle breeze stirs
A bed of gold and silver
Swaying daffodils

The still lake reveals
Another world just beneath
Mirroring this one

Pink petals adrift
Float in the water basin
Advancing summer

Beneath swirling waters
Strobing disco lights, close encounters

Of the hot tub kind

Shimmering starlight
Perhaps someone is out there
Looking back at me

Rolling river mist
Drifts across glassy waters
Silver darts beneath

Against bitter skies
Metal cars wheeling through space
Accompanied by gulls

Soft blue mist curling
Drifting through dense foliage
Aroma of fire

Hey there mister mouse
Hiding under the fireplace
Don't burn your whiskers

Outside my window
Blackbird trilling like a phone
Trolling like a pro

This boiling lobster
By formal Buddhist teachings
Could be my grandma

Sweet scent of springtime
Embarrassment of beauty
Apple blossom blush

Relaxing mindful breaths
A soothing meditation
Blissful purring cat

They were here before
And will endure long after
The Earth is theirs. Trees

Wheeling in blue skies
Dancing with summer's approach
House martins return

Powder petal snow
Falls from cloudless azure skies
Beneath the Rowan

Bursting rosy buds
Roseaceous red petals

Hawthorn in flower

Through the drifting mists
Hopeful holiday makers
Searching for sun beams

Simple honest truth:
Life is mostly nutrition
Some inhalation

A playwrite once said
Better to have loved and lost
All the world's a stage

Birds serenade Strauss
As a warm breeze gently stirs
A flower meadow

What a sight they make
These preening prancing peacocks
Models without pants

The buzz of insects
Delicate flower meadow
Bee rated resort

Though I walk for miles
He never seems much nearer
The pale daylight moon

Black clad mourners weep
At the solemn graveside
A blackbird singing

Preparing coffee
Hands in hot soapy water
Heron watching koi

"It's coming home"
A pigs bladder kickabout
Tribal politics

On roadside verges
Resplendent ruby flowers
Blazing red poppies

Undulating glints
Golden sunlight garnished waves
Gulls soaring above

A convoy of cars
Beneath sunny azure skies

Heading for the coast

A sea breeze stirring
Lifting crying gulls aloft
Above the grey waves

Arms slowly flailing
They march across the skyline
Wind turbine giants

On fast country roads
Motor cyclists overtake
As organ donors

The flitting flower
Seen defying gravity
Is a butterfly

Mowing the garden
In a thirty degree blaze
The haze of summer

Alarming to see
When the power goes off
How many don't know the code

Lateral flow test
For the COVID infection
Was made in China

Arseholes and elbows
Do the power companies
Know the difference?

A day in the sun
Such frail and transient beauty
Is gone tomorrow

Early morning dark
Young ladies totter home drunk
In crumpled dresses

After the night out
Staggering home in disgrace
Drunk and regretful

In early darkness
Young men propped against walls
In drunken slumber

They slumber soundly
So untroubled by life's woes

Simple, honest stones

Sat gathering dust

Unused gym apparatus

Convenient clothes horse

My mind remembers

Days of boundless energy

That my legs forgot

These bravest young men

Return to their mother's arms

In wooden caskets

After the long night

I awake to the new day

Full of aches and pain

Afterword

Thank you for taking the time and trouble to read this book.

It is my sincere hope that you found heart, wisdom and wit between these pages, that you were moved to tears or laughter.

I hope that it imparted on you some small fraction of the joy and pleasure it brought me to compose the verses and put together the work you hold in your hands.

If any of the haiku resonated with you then I would be humbled and grateful if you might take the time to give a review on Amazon or Goodreads. You may also be interested in the companion volume, Haiku Dreams, which contains detailed annotations and beautiful images to accompany the verses, arranged by theme.

Again, thank you for indulging me.

About the Author

Jason Hanrahan lives in Yorkshire, UK, with his partner, two cats and an indeterminate number of koi. He is a software developer with twenty-five years experience and has worked on projects for a host of household names. In his spare time, he cultivates bonsai, loves cinema, and reads Eastern philosophy and literature.

Printed in Great Britain
by Amazon

79358759R00058